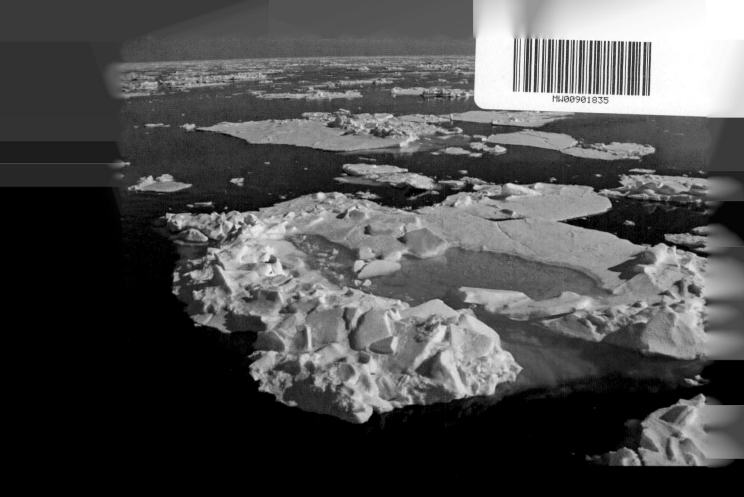

SVALBARD

AN ARCTIC ADVENTURE

by Robert L Ozibko

A barren and frozen land located between 74 and 81 degrees of latitude north, the Svalbard archipelago is one of the world's largest areas of untouched natural beauty. It is filled with majestic mountaintops and dramatic glaciers cascading into the polar ice cap. A land where the midnight sun shines 24 hours a day during the summer months and where darkness obscures the landscape throughout the winter, only to be broken by the eerie glow of the Northern Lights. This is a land of silence and peaceful existence.

ISBN-13: 978-1463530426

Printed in the United States of America.

INTRODUCTION

Dream of a silent and mysterious world draped in white, its jagged peaks enshrouded by eternal snow jutting up from the coastline like a giant saw. Imagine a place where the sun never sets, shining in what seems like an eternal lamp of incandescent fire. Envision a melancholic world of total darkness for half of the arctic year. Picture an endless sea covered with glittering ice as far as the eye can see. A land where the polar bear is king, walking through the endless ice fields in search of the elusive seal to stay alive. Think of immense icebergs, with elegant shapes that challenge the imagination, floating aimlessly on a dark blue sea and casting their silhouettes in magnificent reflections. Visualize pack ice of frozen ocean extending all the way to the North Pole. Listen to deep blue alpine glaciers calving thunderously like giant landslides of frozen rocks. Imagine an environment so intensely powerful and at the same time so vulnerable and fragile. Think of relaxed and sleepy seals resting peacefully on a chunk of drifting ice. Imagine a myriad of birds flying in unison in perfect formation and the ubiquitous reindeer grazing freely on the moist and nutritious tundra. Imagine summer flowers eager to live their ephemeral existence. Think about a pack of walruses lazily sunning themselves in the midnight sun after gorging on the abundant arctic fish colonies. This arctic dream is Svalbard!

HISTORY

Far above the Arctic Circle, between the Barents Sea and the Arctic Ocean, lies a frozen, remote, and mountainous archipelago. Barely 600 miles south of the North Pole, this territory is the largest wilderness of Europe. It is a pristine and enchanting land of dramatic proportions.

After discovery by the Dutch explorer Willem Barents in 1596, this group of islands was occupied by different nations and had no flag until the Treaty of Spitsbergen in 1920, when it became part of the territory of Norway. Barents had named these islands Spitsbergen, a Dutch word meaning "pointed peaks," in reference to the unusual and jagged mountain formation characteristic of this land. After officially taking possession of the islands, Norway renamed its new territory Svalbard, for an old Viking word meaning "cold coast" or "cold rim."

Svalbard, a high arctic archipelago containing approximately 23,900 square miles, is governed by Norway. The area is sparsely populated by groups of different nationalities dedicated to many diverse activities. Mining is among the prime enterprises of the archipelago. Longyearbyen, named after John Longyear, an American miner, is the hub of the Norwegian government activities and Barentsburg, with a population of about 500, is the center of Russian mining operations. Ny-alesund, with almost 100 inhabitants, is a Norwegian research center. The Norwegians also run a mining community in Sveagruva, near Longyearbyen. A team of some 10 Polish scientists operates a research station in Hornsund. Although all this territory is under the jurisdiction of Norway, the laws and the tax structure of Svalbard are localized and different from those of the mainland. The territory is strictly regulated by the Svalbard treaty signed in 1920 by some 40 countries.

5

The largest island in the archipelago retained the name of Spitsbergen, although arriving passengers at the Longyearbyen airport are greeted by an oversize sign that reads SVALBARD. Longyearbyen is the principal and largest community in Spitsbergen and in the entire Svalbard archipelago. Furthermore, it is the only official point of entry to this territory. The city boasts the particular distinction of being the northernmost city in the world.

Traditionally a long-time popular destination for fishermen and hunters, Longyearbyen has become the center of activity for all the commerce and tourism in the archipelago. A relatively small village of little over 1,800 inhabitants, it is surprisingly well stocked with all the necessary elements to support the thriving tourist industry. Post office, banks, modern and comfortable hotels, restaurants, a supermarket, a local newspaper, a small university, and a wonderful science museum are all within walking distance of each other. The airport is small, yet modern, and is only a few minutes from the center of town.

Approximately 60% of the entire archipelago is glaciated — although this figure may vary due to global warming. Thirty percent consists of barren rock and the remaining 10% sustains some kind of vegetation, mostly tundra. It is here where the majority of the birds, foxes, and other terrestrial animals — some permanent residents, some migratory — make their home and breed during the summer season. The pinnipeds, polar bears, whales, and the rest of the Arctic Ocean inhabitants depend on the water for their survival.

Although most of the region appears to be pristine and untouched — except for the open mine pits around the airport — the archipelago has some serious environmental issues. Many years of whaling, hunting, mining, and fishing have taken their toll in the region.

Modern-day laws have ameliorated some of the environmental problems; however, heavy lobbying still preserves the fishing rights that threaten the entire food chain so important to the survival of the animal and plant population of the islands. The fishing industry, though regulated, is the single most important source of environmental disturbance in Svalbard. It's very unlikely that fishing will be banned soon in the archipelago, not only because of the economic value to Norway and many other nations having fishing rights in the area, but because — unlike mining, road construction, and development in general — the damage caused by the fishing industry is not physically and visually apparent until it is too late. Therefore, fishing continues in the area despite the harm it is causing to the habitat.

Most sea mammals and much of the bird population depend on fish and crustaceans for their survival. In turn, the residue that these animals produce from this food serves as fertilizer to sustain the scant plant growth in this arctic environment. The existence of other animals depends primarily on this growth.

It is not difficult to realize the importance of the food chain in preserving nature. Without control, overfishing can turn a unique and vulnerable environment into a lifeless desert.

A bearded seal appears to be relaxing on top of an ice floe

This polar bear is searching for seals like the one above

THE POLAR BEAR

This is the land where the polar bear is king. Having no natural enemies since bear hunting was banned in 1983, polar bears thrive in an environment abundant with their staple food: the ringed seal. Although polar bears and brown bears look different and live in diverse environments, they are genetically related. The two have been successfully mated in zoos, producing fertile offspring. The polar bear is a direct descendant of the brown bear. Through the years, they have adapted their anatomy, diet, and way of life to the arctic environment. Brown bears are omnivorous while polar bears are, for the most part, carnivorous. Compared to other bears, polar bears have a small head and small ears, and a much longer and stronger neck that allows them to lift heavy animals with little effort. Their feet have evolved into large paws that allow them to balance their weight on the ice, thus permitting them to walk on areas where the ice may be too thin to support their weight. Their huge feet help them paddle through the water when swimming. The sense of smell of the polar bear is several times more powerful than that of a bloodhound. They can smell a kill or a female in estrus from several miles away. The polar bear lives and breeds on or near the pack ice where marine life is abundant, particularly ringed seals. They usually follow the edge of the ice cap where seals normally have their breathing holes.

The polar bear is very intelligent. It will patiently spend hours staking out the exit of the breathing holes and, when the seal emerges for air, it will kill it and bring it onto the ice with a single swat of its paw. Polar bears can break the ice with their hind legs, or pounce with their front legs, in search for prey. Polar bears will also feed on walruses, stranded whales, birds, and fish. Occasionally, in the summer when other food is scarce, they have been observed nibbling at vegetation as the last resort, but they need meat to survive.

A male polar bear in search of its prey

While adult males normally hunt alone, they may hang together with other bears in the summer when food is in short supply, causing low levels of testosterone and thus making the bears more tolerant of each other. Cannibalism can occur in polar bears, but it is believed that this is not food-related; rather, it takes place when adult males kill the offspring of competitor males. A male polar bear can normally weigh 1,300 to 1,600 pounds and live 20 to 25 years. Females are much smaller and can live 25 to 30 years. The bears are powerful swimmers, able to paddle through the water for hundreds of miles looking for prey or in search of a female in estrus. Contrary to common belief, most polar bears are not actually white. In the wild, their coats have a creamy yellowish color due to the presence of algae that stick to their fur when they are in the water. Although polar bears seldom mate with other species of bears in the wild, there was one recorded crossbreed between a female polar bear and a male grizzly. That hybrid was killed in Alaska in 2005.

Because food is available year-round, polar bears do not hibernate (as do their related brown bears), except for pregnant females that spend four to five months in their den to give birth and nurture their young until they are old enough to emerge from the lair. Polar bears give birth to twins and, occasionally, triplets. The cubs' survival is relatively low, depending primarily on the availability of food.

The Spitsbergen area is home to an estimated 2,500 to 4,000 bears. These bears can be very dangerous since they have no fear of man. When food is scarce, they will encroach into human habitat and will approach fearlessly any moving animal, including man. Although hunting polar bears is forbidden, occasionally a polar bear may have to be euthanized when interfering with human activity.

This polar bear watches cautiously as our ship goes by

THE JOURNEY

Following a day-long trip from California, we land at the Oslo airport on a typically cloudy yet rather balmy summer afternoon. A quick stop at Customs, then we walk about 300 feet to the comfort of our hotel where we settle in for the evening after a light meal. We purposely arrive in Oslo a day ahead of schedule to protect our trip from any unforeseen delay that might affect our journey. The next morning we board a superb train from the airport station to the center of Oslo, where we spend the day revisiting a city we have not seen for almost 40 years.

The weather is typically Scandinavian, wet and cloudy. We begin our visit at the waterfront, the hub of the city's activity. We board one of the many sightseeing cruise ships near the Oslo City Hall and take a 2-hour tour of the Oslo Fjord. We pass through narrow sounds, idyllic bays, and a maze of small islands with charming and colorful summer homes surrounded by deep blue water.

Shrimp merchant at the Oslo waterfront

Oslo City Hall

After our cruise, we stroll along the waterfront to admire the many beautiful boats and enjoy the sights and sounds of the activity around us. We come across an old steamer where people are celebrating the boat's 100th anniversary. We are invited onboard to tour the ship and participate in the celebration. In spite of its age, the vessel is in remarkably good shape, recently painted and well maintained, its engine humming harmoniously, ready for the next journey. We are invited to cruise the fjord on a two-hour expedition, but politely decline, knowing we still have many other places to visit before the day is over.

An old truck next to the 100 year-old vessel

Charming and colorful summer homes surrounded by deep blue water

An exhibit of old vehicles near the old steamer provides an opportunity to admire many vintage cars and utility vehicles from years past. A mail truck, a fire engine, and several other colorful and impeccably maintained cars and trucks of another era appear to be guarding the old vessel.

Our next stop is Akershus Castle and Fortress, overlooking the waterfront and Oslo City Hall. This medieval castle, completed in the 14th century, was built to protect Oslo from foreign invaders. A past residence of the royal family, the castle was refurbished at the turn of the 20th century. Its strategic location affords magnificent vistas of the Oslo Fjord, City Hall, and the city center.

We stroll through the city streets until we arrive at Vigeland Sculpture Park, a highlight we remember from our previous visit. This is one of Oslo's most visited places. It exhibits the work of Gustav Vigeland, about 200 sculptures in bronze, granite, and cast iron. The park and open-air museum are a truly magnificent display of artistic talent and creativity.

An old fire engine

A vintage mail truck

Vigeland Sculpture Park is one of Oslo's most visited places. It exhibits the work of Gustav Vigeland, about 200 sculptures in bronze, granite, and cast iron

FRIDAY, JUNE 20

Our actual trip starts with a flight from Oslo to Longyearbyen via Tromso — a three-hour journey. As we approach for landing, we get our first glimpse of the spectacular arctic landscape, a splendid aerial view of the snow-covered peaks, fjords, and valleys surrounding Longyearbyen.

Before boarding the ship, we spend a couple of hours at leisure in this colorful frontier town, meeting its friendly citizens and enjoying the typical Scandinavian architecture of pastel-colored buildings.

We have our first encounter with the area's wildlife: a group of reindeer munching the tender new grass right in the middle of the city. We visit the Svalbard Museum, which contains a superb collection of historical events, 17th-century whaling operations, war stories, and a study of the local fauna, flora, and geology. We are treated to a presentation of the town's mining history.

Aerial view of the spectacular arctic landscape

A splendid aerial view of the snow-covered peaks surrounding Longyearbyen

From the air we can see the distinctive landscape surrounding Spitsbergen

Coastal view around Spitsbergen

Typical Scandinavian architecture of pastel-colored buildings

A summer day in Longyearbyen with still some snow on the ground

A view of Longyearbyen's hillside and the town's church

On a splendid summer day, the view from the center of Spitsbergen is magnificent

A pair of reindeer in the middle of town munching the new tender grass

Peculiar land formation on the Spitsbergen coastline

Panoramic view of Spitsbergen coastline

Our home for the next nine days is the *Akademic Sergey Vavilov*. This Russian research ship is used by European scientists to study various aspects of ocean floor composition and ocean water temperatures. The 385-foot-long vessel is equipped with external stabilizers for maximum comfort, and has a reinforced hull specially designed to navigate through ice. The ship features excellent accommodations and services, including a library well stocked with scientific books, a gym, a sauna, a plunge pool, and presentation rooms. Hosting 110 passengers and 53 crew members, it provides the additional convenience of traveling on a small ship. Navigation takes place, for the most part, in the relatively calm waters of the fjords and the protected channels and bays of the islands. The *Vavilov* is equipped with Zodiacs, exceptionally strong, reinforced, and motorized rubber boats that can carry up to 10 passengers ashore with remarkable speed and safety.

After we board the ship, we are served afternoon tea and pastries by the Russian crew, followed by a welcome briefing and all *de rigueur* drills for safety and comfort aboard and the excursions ashore. The ship's itinerary is very flexible and subject to change depending on weather conditions, animal sightings, and other circumstances that will improve our journey. After dinner, we begin to get used to the midnight sun which, at this latitude, never sets below the horizon between April 19 and August 23.

SATURDAY, JUNE 21

Today is the longest day of the year. We receive more safety lectures and general information briefings prior to boarding the Zodiacs for our first excursion ashore. We are not allowed to disembark until an armed patrol — our guides — lands first. Armed with high-power rifles for protection, they scout the area to ensure that no polar bears are in the vicinity. This will be the norm throughout the trip. All persons venturing into the wilderness areas of the Svalbard archipelago are advised to carry firearms for protection against possible encounters with polar bears. Therefore, the guides are always armed during our hikes and at least one of them is strategically positioned on a high point, near the shore, constantly vigilant for bears.

On our first venture ashore, we visit Hornsund Fjord, a splendid sound with stunning views of the mountain chain and astonishing glacial formations. We come upon amazingly beautiful icebergs with a myriad of shapes and sizes resembling ethereal sculptures. We make a relatively long trek up the mountain, partly on the snow, partly on the tundra, to observe a colony of dovekies (aka little auks), a sociable arctic bird. The scenery is breathtaking and the feeling exhilarating. We are surrounded by the peaceful magnificence of the arctic landscape. It is our first experience walking on the tundra, which is comparable to walking on a mattress, soft and fluffy. The dovekies seem to have fun flying in perfect formation and landing with flawless precision on the rocky nesting area. A group of Polish research scientists stationed on the sound, near the dovekie colony, is dedicated to observing and studying these birds and other scientific activities. In addition to the dovekie, we see barnacle geese, reindeer, arctic fox, and an array of lovely spring flowers such as yellow and purple saxifrage, mountain avens, and roseroot. Colorful lichens amid the flowers complement the wonderful psychedelic landscape.

We take a relatively long trek up the mountain surrounding Hornsund Fjord to visit a colony of dovekies. We hike partly on snow and partly on the tundra.

We come upon amazingly beautiful icebergs with a myriad of shapes and sizes resembling etherial sculptures

The elegant shapes of these icebergs can challenge the imagination

These dovekies fly continuously from the colony to the water, where they feed and collect food for their young

A pair of dovekies resting on a rock

The ubiquitous reindeer seems to tolerate our presence with apparent ease

Highland saxifrage

Purple saxifrage

Mountain avens

Roseroot

29

SUNDAY, JUNE 22

Today we reach the southern tip of Spitsbergen, then steam north along the pack ice in search of polar bears. As we proceed north, the ice becomes heavier and the ocean turns rough, with high swells. The winds, producing gusts of up to 50 miles per hour, cause enormous waves to break over the bow. Ironically, our program for the day begins with a quotation by J. Lamont; "Nothing can exceed the sublime grandeur of a really fine day in these regions." The weather does not allow any outside activity, hence we spend most of the day studying in the ship's well-stocked library and enjoying educational programs. We listen to Dr. Ian Stirling's outstanding lecture, "The Natural History and Ecology of the Polar Bear." Dr. Stirling is the best known and most respected polar bear researcher in the world. We also spend part of the time developing new friendships with our fellow passengers. After dinner, Dr. Gary Alt presents a fascinating and amusing talk entitled "A Lighthearted Look at Bears and Biologists," in which he candidly relates some of the most hilarious and unusual experiences he had as a young researcher.

As we retire for the day, the midnight sun is hidden behind the clouds of the Arctic Ocean and the stormy skies project an eerie feeling of loneliness. We drift along the empty ocean and into the world of dreams, a world as large as our imagination can fathom.

Our ship at anchor on one of the fjords

Glaucous gulls resting on an iceberg

MONDAY, JUNE 23

On the fourth day of our journey, the thermometer reads 2°C (35.6°F). The weather is absolutely perfect, sunny without a gust of wind. A few cloud formations adorn the deep blue sky with spectacular velvety shapes. The ocean is smooth as silk and the panorama truly magnificent. A European swallow and three-crossed beak, birds native to continental Europe and apparently pushed north of the continent by the storm, are clinging desperately to our ship in search of warmth, food, and rest from a long and arduous flight. We hope they survive.

The Zodiacs take us on a ride through the drifting ice. The ocean is calm as a lake and the towering icebergs, like giant ghostly figures, create a surreal panorama. We navigate the frozen ocean landscape in the midst of imposing ice sculptures and marvelous reflections. The air is crisp, the arctic silence broken only by the occasional delicate song of a bird or the almost imperceptible sound of breaking ice. The frozen sculptures, surrounded by brilliant emerald pools, cast enchanting mirror images on a magical arctic ocean. The entire mythical panorama inspires an indescribable feeling of exhilaration and peace. We do not want to leave. We want to preserve this moment for the rest of our lives. Eventually, reality sets in. It is time to return to the ship.

This afternoon we approach Edgeoya Island, still looking for polar bears. We encounter more majestic ice floes casting their magic reflections, and a myriad of birds flying overhead. Some of the floes are filled with birds resting or preening themselves. Others are drifting by with a seal as a passenger. A black guillemot takes a bath nearby, oblivious to our presence. Our surroundings are silent and serene, inspiring a mood of total bliss.

Our post-dinner talk tonight is "Stories from the Arctic" by Gordon Court, a collection of amusing anecdotes and personal experiences. Before bedtime, we sit on the deck of the ship and reminisce on the wonderful moments experienced during the day. With the sun still shining high in the sky, we turn in, wishing we could slow down the clock in order to enjoy these moments a bit longer.

A European swallow and a crossed-beak take refuge on our ship in search or warmth, food and rest after a storm pushed them north of the mainland

The Zodiacs take us on a picturesque ride through the drifting ice

A flock of black guillemots frolic playfully in the water around a small iceberg

The towering icebergs, like ghostly figures, create a surreal panorama

We encounter more majestic ice floes casting their magic reflections on the ocean

Our guide scans the horizon in search of wildlife

A pair of northern fulmars rest on the water among ice floes

TUESDAY, JUNE 24

Today the *Vavilov* steams along the southeast coast of Spitsbergen Island next to the pack ice in search of the elusive polar bear. In the process, we visit Kvalvagen, Hambergbreen, and Isbukta Fjords. We soon spot a large male polar bear swimming vigorously along the edge of the ice and away from our ship. It has a big number 8 painted on its rump, indicating that it has been captured at least once, and probably carries an electronic monitoring device to track its activities. It's obvious that this bear is aware of the ship, perhaps associating our vessel with its previous capture, because he suddenly climbs onto the ice and starts running away from us at full speed, glancing back with apprehension.

We pass several bearded seals resting comfortably on an ice floe, apparently indifferent to the ursine danger around them. Black guillemots are flying in perfect formation all around us while a northern fulmar is vigorously flapping its wings in the water, taking its daily bath. Minke whales cavort happily ahead of our vessel. Once more, we venture among the drift ice aboard our Zodiacs to admire the frigid arctic panorama.

Back on the *Vavilov*, Peggy Abbot, one of the naturalists aboard, delivers a lecture on "Assembling the Arctic," an interesting narrative concerning the animal population and the arctic habitat. Afterward, Dr. Wayne Petersen, an avian expert from the Audubon Society, discusses "The Natural History of Seabirds." The final activity of the day features Dr. Ian Peterson entertaining us with a comical dissertation on why a polar bear biologist can't get insurance.

Bear number 8 runs away from our vessel glancing back from time to time with apparent apprehension

This bear is trying to maintain equilibrium on the melting ice

Wary of our ship, these polar bears watch us with caution

Dovekies in flight

Bearded seal resting on an ice floe

Northern fulmar taking a bath

Black guillemot

WEDNESDAY, JUNE 25

On day six, we are awakened at three o'clock in the morning to admire the beauty of the Samarinvaagen Fjord, surrounded by jagged mountains and wintry glaciers. The scenery is breathtaking. The water is motionless and silky smooth, the reflections spectacular. The air is still, the views inspiring and stimulating. This serene and magnificent white kingdom is magical. We contemplate the idyllic panorama with a sense of awe. I begin to photograph this terrestrial paradise, not realizing that the ecstatic feeling of the moment cannot be captured in an image.

In the afternoon, we hike around Berzellstinden, a relatively flat bay where we find a small cetacean cemetery with noticeable skeletal remains. The area contains several shallow ponds where red-necked phalaropes feast on summer flies. We pause and observe the entire panorama, the birds and a few reindeer, the soggy and delicate tundra, and the remnants of whales. We feel the chilly arctic wind on our faces and suddenly realize how fortunate we are to be able to witness the natural, exquisite, untamed beauty of the arctic. I swiftly grab the fleeting splendor of the moment, albeit ephemeral, and forever store it in my mind.

Back on the ship, we conclude another wonderful day in this arctic Eden with a dynamic lecture by Dennis Mense on "The Evolution of Small Ship Expeditions and Forays into the Far East."

Zodiac surrounded by pack ice and the *Vavilov* in the background

Spectacular reflections on the Samarinvaagen Fjord

A panoramic view of Samarinvaagen Fjord

A glacier casts reflections on silky-smooth water

Ice floes, blue water, a glaciated coastline, and jagged peaks create a distinct frozen panorama

A sheet of fractured ice, with bear tracks, covers most of the ocean panorama

A cetacean cemetery in Berzellstinden bay contains years of accumulated skeletal remains

The spine of a deceased whale is well preserved by the Arctic weather

Parasitic jaeger on its nest

Red-necked phalarope feasting on summer flies

Black guillemot

Snow bunting

THURSDAY, JUNE 26

Though already into the seventh day of our journey, we continue to be awed by the sheer beauty of the arctic landscape. Shortly after breakfast, we board the Zodiacs to visit Blomstrandhalvoya, near Ny-Alesund. We land near a former marble quarry founded by Ernest Mansfield, an enthusiastic English entrepreneur. We climb a hill from where we have magnificent vistas of Konsfjord. Farther up hill, the tundra turns into a flourishing garden of wildflowers and other small plants. The area is teeming with wildlife. A herd of a dozen reindeer watches with suspicion as we approach. They finally accept our presence and continue grazing. Several arctic terns and parasitic jaegers are comfortably nesting on the ground, while a rock ptarmigan and a snow bunting peck contentedly at the new plant growth. As we approach, the terns and the jaegers chase us away from their territory by noisily squawking, dive-bombing, and pecking our heads.

In the afternoon, we visit the 14th of July Glacier, with a stopover at a series of cliffs which serve as nesting grounds for Atlantic puffins, thick-billed murres, and the ubiquitous sea gulls. I have seen many glaciers in Alaska, Canada, Argentina, and Chile. However, this magnificent glacier in Krossfjord introduces a new experience to my previous observations. The ice is crowded with a multitude of birds and seals dozing on top of chunks of floating ice calved from the glacier. As we land for a hike around the glacier, we encounter a meadow alive with summer growth. The deep green color of the tundra contrasts sharply with the black rock formations. A diverse assortment of wildflowers, such as mountain avens, moss campion, and draba, forms a luxuriant garden and provides nesting grounds and food for arctic terns, jaegers, and geese.

We climb up a hill where we observe fabulous vistas of Konsfjord

Remnants of a former marble quarry

Not even this remote region of the Arctic can escape human intrusion

A herd of reindeer watches cautiously as we approach their territory

Only a few shacks remain of the former marble quarry

A parasitic jaeger stands guard next to its nest

A rock ptarmigan changing into summer plumage is pecking the new growth

An arctic tern is guarding its colony

An arctic tern lets out a warning scream at approaching intruders

A brief visit to a cliff that serves as nesting grounds for Atlantic puffins, thick-billed murres, and sea gulls.

Ivory gull guarding its nest

Atlantic puffin

Atlantic puffins

Black guillemots

Glaucous gulls resting on an iceberg

Sleepy seal on an ice floe next to a glacier

Colorful glacier

A northern fulmar enjoys the Arctic's panorama from above

Photo opportunities abound in this marvelous environment

Seal on an ice floe with the glacier in the background

This zodiac cruises slowly on the calm waters of the ocean while the guests enjoy the panorama

Bearded seal

Zodiac and glaucous gulls sitting on an ice floe

This zodiac is dwarfed by the towering glacier

Green and brown moss

Tufted saxifrage

Yellow arctic whitlow and scurvy grass

Draba

Purple saxifrage

Tundra moss

FRIDAY, JUNE 27

On the eighth day of our expedition, we head for the northernmost point of the trip — 80 degrees of latitude north — off the west coast of Spitsbergen Island, again in search of the polar bear. The ice is about a foot thick on the average, but can be much thicker in some places. As our ship navigates cautiously at a very low speed, the cracking sounds of the breaking ice give us an eerie feeling of helplessness. We are surrounded by the infinite solitude of the Arctic Ocean, with nothing in sight, not a ship, not a sound, except for the cracking ice and our pounding hearts. We are alone. We are at the mercy of nature!

Suddenly, in the seemingly endless expanse of frozen ocean, we spot a pair of walruses serenely dozing on the ice next to a breathing hole. From time to time, they cautiously raise their heads, probing the air and scanning the horizon for possible danger. Unknown to them, a short distance away a large male bear is visibly intrigued by the presence of the walruses. He cunningly and gingerly slides on the ice, sometimes swimming in the water, without a sound, silently working his way around the walruses. As he gets nearer, he glides noiselessly onto the ice so as not to alert his intended prey. Suddenly, the bear appears in front of the walruses, but instead of attacking he observes them curiously for a brief moment, perhaps sizing up his prey. A male walrus can be twice the size of a polar bear. Swiftly, the walruses sit up on the ice and stare at the bear for an instant, then quickly disappear in the water, where the bear has no chance at all of capturing them. We are happy for the walruses.

Meteo Info

Temperature:	-0.5
Pressure:	1017.0
Wind Dir. :	47
Wind speed:	12 m/s
R. humidity:	65 %

GMT:	15:53:16 (+2)
Lat:	7953.338 N
Lon:	01002.439 E
Heading:	226.
Gyro:	217.1
Speed:	04.1 (Kn)

Meteorology data on the ship's computer

The *Vavilov* and pack ice

Two male polar bears, possibly brothers, meander the polar ice cap in search of food

The *Vavilov* inches along the pack ice

Pack ice covers most of the ocean's surface near the polar ice cap

Thin ice forces this polar bear to use caution when walking

Yawning bear

This polar bear exhibits a distinctive yellow hue on its fur due to algae picked up when swimming in the arctic waters

This bear shows less yellow tint than the bear above, possibly because it is a younger bear

SATURDAY, JUNE 28

Today is the last day of our journey. Early in the morning, the Zodiacs take us to Poolepynten, on the east shore of Prins Karls Foreland Island, where we visit a walrus colony. As we approach the sleepy group, we detect a peculiar and strong marine odor characteristic of these animals. They are so packed together that they appear to be positioned one on top of the other. They seem undisturbed by our presence. The only noticeable activity in the group is the sporadic arrival of a new pair of walruses from the sea to join the cluster. The big males are massive, up to 12 feet long, weighing as much as 3,000 pounds, and are armed with a huge pair of tusks that can measure up to three feet in length. Walruses inhabit the shallow waters off the Arctic coast and spend considerable time resting on the pack ice. They dive in shallow waters and use their stiff facial whiskers to feed on mollusks hidden under a muddy or gravelly bottom. They also feed on small fish and other invertebrates. Nearly exterminated by hunters during the 19th century, the walrus population has been slowly increasing since 1952, when they became protected.

In the afternoon, we land at Alkhornet, in Isfjorden, for the last hike of our trip. In addition to the omnipresent reindeer, we find an arctic fox den with a busy female caring for eight pups. Albeit vigilant, she does not seem to be concerned by our presence. We spend several minutes observing how the litter, oblivious to us, consumes a large goose their mother has provided. Several pairs of nesting birds are dive-bombing our group anytime we get too close to their nest.

The day, and our trip, concludes with a farewell cocktail party and the captain's dinner, followed by a slide presentation of our activities during the journey, courtesy of the official ship's photographer.

Our journey has come to an end. However, the dazzling memories of this trip will forever be engraved in our minds. This rich arctic experience was a mix of solitude, exhilaration, and everything in between. The talented group of guides aboard the ship provided an unparalleled and rich learning opportunity and helped us understand a world that, until now, had only existed in the imagination. To experience the Arctic has been a magical and unforgettable experience.

Walrus colony

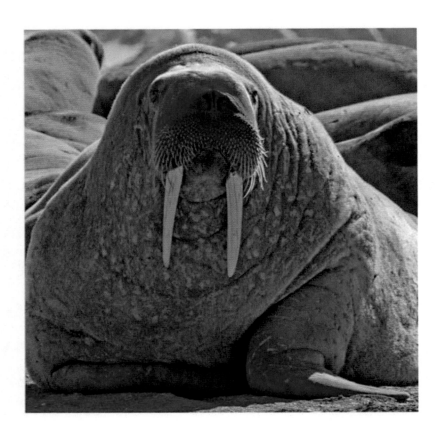

Walrus colony

This arctic fox litter consumes a large goose provided by their mother

This arctic fox female does not seem to be concerned by our presence but is vigilant of other intruders that may invade her territory

Twice a day the zodiacs are deployed and retrieved from the ocean

Photography is an important part of this trip

Our group relaxes and enjoys a splendid, sunny arctic day

After a wonderful day of hiking and learning, evening is all fun at the *Vavilov's* lounge

The author and his wife 600 miles south of the North Pole

ABOUT THE AUTHOR

An engineer by profession and a passionate photographer, Bob Ozibko is a graduate of the School of Modern Photography. He has been dedicated to nature and travel photography for most of his life. His photographs have appeared in *Aquarium magazine, Zoonooz, Photographics, Popular Photography, Nature Photographer, Wonderful Wetlands,* The International Library of Photography, and many travel catalogs. He travels extensively around the United States and the world to capture the best of nature. His favorite subjects are wildlife, people, and landscapes. Bob Ozibko has published more than ten books recounting his many adventures around the world, all of them illustrated by his award-winning photographs.

Made in the USA
Coppell, TX
20 July 2023

19370102R00052